During an historical period of time in Oakland California, Mary Rudge, as part of an emerging small press movement, brought out limited editions of chapbooks and edited or co-edited anthologies, often handbound, which became collectors' items. Among these are: "Spirit Woods"; "The Fringe: A Mexican Journal"; "Struck Lodestone"; "From the Heart of the Bay"; "Oakland is a Holy City"; "Bus Poems"; "Blue Haiku and Short Poems"; "Poems for Ireland"; "Ipagpatawad Ninyo Kami" (with Amy Estrada); "Collage of Wild Leaves" (with Claire Baker); and "Maps for Poets" (published in India).

Anthologies include: "Dreaming of Wings" (co-edited with Natasha Borovsky, Florence Miller, and Elaine Starkman); "Think All the Light" (co-edited with Maggi Meyer); "State of Peace: The Women Speak" (Gull Press, New York; co-edited with Natasha Borovsky, Florence Miller and Elaine Starkman); "Peace Poems by Children"; "Poets and Peace International" (co-edited with Maggi Meyer); "Reaping" (a tribute anthology for the farmworkers); "Alameda's First Anthology of Poetry and Drawings"; and ". . . as many as oakleaves: POETS IN OAKLAND".

The Oakland anthology, "To Build a Fire", published in 1976 by Mark Ross, contained these words by editor Floyd Salas:

"How many of you can tell me who were the star baseball players of 1916 when Jack London died? Yet everyone remembers him all over the world . . . In a city that has produced geniuses like Jack London and Gertrude Stein . . . there is the hard work and genius of Mary Rudge, one of the finest and purest poets I know."

WATER PLANET

POEMS BY MARY RUDGE

with a preface by
Leopold Sedar Senghor

GATEWAY ARTS • OAKLAND

Gateway Arts
A nonprofit public benefit corporation
PO Box 3267, Oakland CA 94609

Library of Congress Number 85-51148
ISBN 0-935327-00-2

Poems in this collection have appeared in *La Vida Cultural; Poema Convidado; Compages; Nueva Alcarria* (Guadalajara, Spain); *Napa Review; Women Talking/Women Listening; Wordhustlers; Berkeley Poets Cooperative/16; Bay Area Poets Coalition Anthologies; Alameda Poets Anthologies; Poet* (published in India); *California Living; Alameda Times-Star;* and numerous other publications.

Cover illustration by Susan Seddon Boulet, by permission of the artist. Susan Seddon Boulet's work was used for the jacket design of Volume 5 of the *Diary of Anais Nin* (Harcourt, Brace, Janovich), and for the cover of *Dancing the Naked Dance of Love* by Barbara Gravelle (Archangel Books).

Photo of the poet by Jordan.

Typesetting donated by Bu Wirth and Consolidated Capital Equities Corporation.

We are grateful to Sally Abbott, Richard Angilly, Estelle Jelinek, Helen Malkerson, and Suzanne Miller for donating time to this book.

Manufactured in the United States of America

First edition

10 9 8 7 6 5 4 3 2 1

PREFACE

Mary Rudge was an active member of the American delegation to the 7th World Congress of Poets that I presided over last year in Marrakech, the poetic city in the center of Morocco.

The collection she gives us here is characteristic both of American art and twentieth century poetry, what we defined in Marrakech as "one or more analogous, melodious, and rhythmical images." Indeed, ever since the Revolution of 1889, marked by Henri Bergson's essay *The Immediate Data of Consciousness*, the United States has had an important role in shaping the twentieth century esthetic, especially in poetry, music and dance.

What is striking about Mary Rudge's collection is that it reveals her soul which embraces not only the people of America, but also the people and lands of the ancient Mediterranean world. Happily, the 8th World Congress of Poets will be held in Greece this year, in the country which took the torch of civilization, especially poetry, from the hands of Egypt in the 5th century B.C. And Mary Rudge will be there to celebrate the earth and the sea, the sun and the moon, Morocco, Ireland, France, Persia, and lands as far away as Bangladesh. But above all, through rhythm and dance, she will salute all people, all races, all tongues, and the great American melting pot which forecasts the *Universal Civilization* that will exist at the dawning of the next millennium.

All of the poems in this collection are woven from certain symbols and images. Here, splendid and radiant, are those of the first verse of the first poem.

We who are luminous,
are radiant,

are 90% light,
who know a fiery fusion that
makes stars and suns,
whose flesh is compressed of dancing atoms,

And here are the analogous images, familiar and sensual:

roads through the valley
are mostly orange
smell of orange   and when it rains   the roads
are juice, and avocado pulp,
lemon, sticky   with orange,   sweet
sweet orange roads
with juice of honeydew melons seed spit out
and odor of cantaloupe,
grapefruit smell upon my flesh

"Sensual Landscape." How the title rings true! Everywhere rhythm is king, as in "Aliyah":

Men in woven robes,
children of brown bare limbs,
women with tambourines,
guiding their ewes and lambs,
walking, calling out, singing,
talking, dancing, clapping their hands.

As you can see, this is a rhythm formed by asymmetrical parallelism, by repetitions that do not repeat exactly. It is stronger still in "For Women in Fringed Shawls," which is so rhythmic it compels a dance and in fact is dedicated "to Natica who choreographed this poem."

This poem, with its choreography, is most significant. It is here that our poet, with all the New World, returns to the origins of humanity and its art, to *Poiesis*, which meant artistic creation to the ancient Greeks. She returns to ancient Egypt, to Mother Africa, where the same word means poetry, song and dance.

Leopold Sedar Senghor
Paris, France; July 19, 1985

CONTENTS

Water Planet

WE WHO ARE LUMINOUS

We who are luminous,
        are radiant,
are 90% light,
who know a fiery fusion that
makes stars and suns,
whose flesh is compressed of
        dancing atoms,

we chart an inner astronomy
our nucleus, our energy,
without burning our eyes,
we see.

There is a crust of seasons that we wear.
Seeds sleep along the bones, erupt, and bloom
in heats and darks responsive to our moon.
Flames loop and leap the arteries,
there is a core of ember in the womb—
      beyond our brightness
      our creation, cells,
   connect in constellations of our own.

YES!

Here I am yes on the verge
but barely, yes on the brink of knowing
what it was I could not grasp; the hand so close
to the, what is it core, pit, rind,
that it could not clasp but a moment before
the transient thought and time on the verge
of passing, a second too late,
the mind hangs down like
                    plantain leaves, a pouch
of dreams—vague—yes   here I am
on the verge
                    this moment. Minute speck,
making my presence secure with a poem,
a few cave-lines of the woolly mammoth
is all his existence now.

Here I am on the ridge
      of the day's break, the edge of dawn.
The watering of vines that makes these
mornings glorious with blue bloom is all
my concern, remembering   yes   it was
in our care.
I don't know why those others left, I heard,
rocketing off into space
forgetting the twining of arms and the
turning of face for the kiss mattered,
or that there were squirrels at the window
and seagulls swooping the air.
They didn't say,
as they invented the tools for the wars
                    —and see that
overgrown jungle heap collection
of obsolete technological things they junked
there,   here on the edge of
a new world.

I'm in the garden, yes, here
on the verge of knowing,
well, and the snake coiled yesterday
on the tree branch with a
tongue-slithering smile.

And I, on the verge of passing
over almost the world's rim,
in my knowledge of quick time, how so little
it took for the goblet, the hemlock—oblivion
of the collected facts. I am inking my lips
and my fingertips blackberry juice red
seeing the markings that follow on all I touch.
Here I am yes on the verge
a little too late, or too soon, for the
cadence completing the thought.

POEM FOR DROWNED CHILDREN

Newspaper headlines, on the
empty airplane seat beside me,
flowed their inky waves across the page;
"Crying, the children were swept away."*
Wave, that welled up as just another wave,
turned Tsunami on the Kamoasa shore.
There was no warning rush or roar,
so quiet it took the children,
then smoothed out unmoved,
leaving parents racing down the beach,
their screams and moans lost in the day,
      to huddle at the rocks and weep of love.

Water, have you not all that is wonderful
to hug and hold for long eternal drift,
that these hands, marked with
               ripple lines of palm
and tiny whorl of tips of fingers petaled out
as underwater flowers, bloom
below the glow of luminescent surface
      ringed with diatoms?

Do they float in deep-lying Kuroshio current,
long channel's frigid vagaries?
Swing with the sun's great circular orbits,
with diagonal shifts of winds,
where cold light bends?
In depths too slow for the foot's loose dance?

They are not as they were before,
mouths open to sand and salt,
their laughter leaping about them like smooth
                                                silver fish.

Their hair will be combed with thin backbones
          of neckless creatures,
          in some cold sink's dense decay,
or they sway, organic, nutrient,
fertile with phosphates   when
tides nourish birds, whose beaks touch beaks
  of their reflections, and fish in splashy cycles
  ring the big gong of the moon.
I, in that plane-flight
followed white foam patterns
that slid under watery sky
far below wavy clouds,
not knowing which was cloud
and which was wave-crest
where children's   small spirits floated by my
window   through the air.   There,
                    Heavenward   through   the air.

**Story by Lewis M. Simons, The Mercury, San Jose, May 27, 1983.*

REMEMBERING ATLANTIS

I will begin with
the wall's mural in motion.
Purple ripples awash on it.
Air bubbles on my lips a long time.
    There are no new words to describe
    subterranean existence.
If you don't know what it was like
in Atlantis before, you will not remember
this poem.

The elongate waves of sound
    overlay through water.
Hear in the bones,
    currents of thought. In water swinging
        our voices. Sonar.
The dark is very green.
Noon-rays of sun shaft through thick ocean
on shape of conch-shell mosque.

    Visiting Assyrians east of the city,
    encamped on the outskirts,
    in centuries moved no closer.
    Fissures had opened, for their tents,
        floating thin pennants.
    Their rusted swords, secret in shreds of robes
    (shroud-like, tissue sheer) close
        to their webbed hands.
    Those that survive plunge in the dark,
        on stallions
    with hooves green mold.

    In pavilion's shadows their women wait,
    Near treasure of sunken ship-hold.
    Old coins jangle at their hips on gold chains

Wound round and around.
They will not exchange them for
anything. More precious than shells
their finger cymbals.
The dancing girl
kicks on the pillows her tinkling anklets.

On the left bank of water that flows to all water,
poets, by tradition
gathered each year to bring words from all
nations,
writers, translators, searching an alchemy
that turns "injustice" and "hunger" and "anger"
into the word PEACE—whose lives
in an instant became new element.
Water takes all words into itself.

Princes came in disguise
to have ordinary moments,
transformed by liquid
they free-flow the streaming streets
equal to sturgeon and marlin and porpoise.

Here stone erodes, algae covered walls,
filled bowls and pottery. The statues crumble.

Children tried to hide at first.
Where can you hide
from water
which seeps in the pores?
It came under doors,
in open windows.
It filled the air.

There are no hours or years that are not watery.
Why did not the strong of us swim upward
or pull ourselves to the surface and sing?
There is nothing we wanted, ever, that is not here.

For a long time we breathed a mingled air
in the porous buildings
or in pockets of earth. When liquid entered—
we reached transition.
For a long time we ate fragments from
clay pots in wet ash of ovens
and hardly knew we began to crave the seaweed.

    Leda   one day
    when the dead swan drifted downward
    said "there are no new visions
    only old myths retold."

Icarus
had such feathers
blue white, billowy,
spiraling
to the whirlpool vortex of volcanoes
and   in slow motion   fire
rose up through the ocean
leaped to be destroyed by drowning.

We live on. Here, a transmuted existence.

    I am priestess of waters
    riding the sacred seahorse
    updown the galloping waves—
    the unborn in his pouch—
    his filmy muzzle
    nuzzles fields of wet things—
    my hair, palomino mane, floats along
        foam crest.

My love who writes my praises
wakes on the dais
with his water pipe,
musing; Unsubstantiated substance,

an uncorked jinn   up from the bottle
floating in and out of windows tends him.
Water has washed off our masks,
               washed out our tears.
We have grown fins on our forearms, gills
               at the throat,
in the dark water   blue green glows   in the
               black light those eyes—
(Phosphorescence.
We touch
no longer flesh
but not quite scale)
transparencies wet glisten.

Over the waters came skimming the singing birds,
               after Atlantis
               the ark
               entered through arc of the rainbow
               a new testament.
My love tells in ghazal what he thinks of me now.
(There are no new words for love.)
          There is no new way to tell
            something so old
               so ancient.

Ghazal: Persian verse pattern.

PRAISE POEM

(written in Morocco)

What if I ruled water
in a world where men rule men?
Who commands irrigation and aquaducts
holds life and death in his hand.

To establish my domain
I'd know water's dangerous games,
    exile wild waves to oceans—
        the Atlantic off Casablanca—
            imprison it for its salt,
                destroyer of root
                                    of leaf.
Demand that it be pure
    upon the plain, as stream
        of my own consciousness
                claim it and reclaim.

What if the sun—that spy
    is force. Strong enemy
    that hammers the land all day.
    What if the land is clay
    and earth can only be as dust
    in defeat, at my feet.
I would form alliance with water
    let it reflect the sun's red eye
    back on itself until
    ashamed it lowers its gaze
        and lays its weapon down
        in the heat-red haze,
and the water shimmers its ecstasy
                                                        for me.

I would call it to dance—
        let fountain and spray mist be its veils—

to charm the granite, the hard rock
and move freely through mountains
and hills.

I would declare a festival. The people
could come dressed as clouds
and there would be real clouds in the sky. I'd
call all—even the smallest child
to receive such riches of rain
drops like diamonds to lay on their hands,
their fingers would wear the dew.
We would sign a treaty with sun
never more to be enemy.
See the moon with her tides at her hem
admire me for ending the wars—
and every day we would celebrate
peace among the planets
learning the songs of the stars.

The sheep in the new grass
bleat out thanks,
bringing the lambs to graze,
the people who harvest the corn
have joy in my powers
have praise,
glad to be born in this hour.

FOR WOMEN WHO LOVE THE SEA

Do women become impregnated by sea
full of semen of mermen and dead sailors
(wars enough) purple man-o-war testicles
   swollen, or stringy as weeds
   blood of fish cut by rudders
their scales-silver weighed in bank vaults
   of original settlers
         when there were salmon and sturgeon
larger than men in the Estuary,
fish elongated, shaped like tongues
large and small going in and out
obscured by film their mouths
         loosing a million bubbles
sucking in algae glutted with sun,
there are seals that returned to be
         sea creatures again
their haunches strange as our knees
whale parts that contain
fingerbones perfectly formed
and whales who have risen—thrust out,
         and shown
the size of their penis.

Women who love the beaches at night
who go there alone and have heard
someone telling them secrets
incredible beyond bearing
giving themselves to the teller
only stunned at climax crested
half in half out of tide
feeling flipper instead of arm
and seeing departure of dolphin
deep in the dusky water.

So have they used language?
to think they were kept in our laboratories,
tracking our enemy submarines,
Allies, has it come to this?

There are children they say who are not like us
sons and sisters   of Pisces, daughters
of women who've loved the waters
see them floating
through pink-purple streets at dawn
mouths opening and closing against the air
like pale anemone   the multiple shades of
blues and greens on their skins
children who—not like us—
        see concrete complexes sinking
        say; let oceans take back tidelands
        the Bay become a Sanctuary.

Whenever that cold spray hits my lip
and I taste the tears in its salt
feel the urgency
in the slow sure pull of the Estuary,
even when my own reflection
shimmers on still wet sidewalks
I feel the flesh compressed in that invisible sea—
I ask then was it there
        this generation was spawned—

DANCE WITH WHALES

You have no choice but drown
        or dance with whales!
   Down the spume trail steep
   sea mammals go—
        and sleep   and wake   and rise
break out of water's darkness—loom and turn!
Flukes raised to salute the sun—fins
hold forgotten bones of our fingers that
          ache no more   for land.

     Air keeps our breath's warm steam
and the fling of our bodies to space
in the dance between two elements—
but, below, all the waters know
               our ecstasy of song.
               Hear how our poems resound
in the inarticulate deep.

Come join us! When shores open   and let you go.
     When the tidal wave grasps earth.
                         You have   no choice
     but drown
               or move with the infinite flow—

                  or move in the infinite flow—

                              drown
                      or dance with whales!

SOUND IN AMBER
(FOR SOME COLD
SOME FROZEN FUTURE MORNING
THE SUN REFUSES TO WARM,
CENTERED IN MY HEART,
EARTH.)

From the valley of Ourika, Morocco,
I brought this amber bead,
ancient sand speck, dust mote,
minute insect (maybe its note
of music still within),
these centuries unchanged—

I see myself the same—
poem in my mouth, suspended in time
moment of trumpet call solidifies
sound,   some morning held in amber.

THE POET'S WORK

The Poet's work is this geography
overlaid with lines which cross a page
and—as directions told in foreign tongue
with meanings slightly changed—guide on.
I was once—when I was there—
    have been where—
becomes part—if just a pause
before dropping coins on the counter for
another ticket in a bus station,
following those lights
taken from small gold boxes,
that would hold the lemony sun of Spain.
Or, marked with tracks for the night coach
(stopped in Belgium, students, on the floor
with sleeping bags, who shuttle all their summer
between Amsterdam and France).
Or, on waters where canal boats'
orange geraniums' fragmented flowers
swimming ducks' feet scatter into ripples as
ink drips
from tips
of our fingers, in our trails through Holland,
as we smile our mornings at each other.
We tell of dream routes
between wake and rising
the mind wanders.

How slow thoughts emerge as continents
        through time,
or place after place seen in succession,
and the suitcase filled with journals
in the strange room's closet
is opened and closed on the next vision
as verse follows verse,
as bridges over rivers soon forgotten.

How the lines connect,
the interlocking pattern across surfaces
ascending into sky's planes for the flight
that began from Eden
and relates the planets to our lives
and yet uncharted countless trace of stars,
across the endless map which is the poem.

ALIYAH
(a going up)

Jerusalem, Jerusalem,
to you the tribes
(from centuries long gone)
go up.
Still almost in our vision
we dream them so strongly.

Men in woven robes,
children of brown bare limbs,
women with tambourines,
guiding their ewes and lambs,
walking, calling out, singing,
talking, dancing, clapping their hands.
  Single file from the narrow pass,
  through the mountains,
  scar-marked feet in those thick sandals,
  skin sun darkened.
Follow the ram's horn, across hot desert.
            ALIYAH!
            ALIYAH!
Under the bulbs of cupolas, minaret's tower,
through dark back alleys,
past the pool of Hezekiah—
                  Jerusalem, Jerusalem,
                  the tribes go up.
Go with their cameras and sunglass cases
    over narrow streets
    in unsuitable shoes.
The ones so young they come
because their parents say
            "come!"
Those who come alone from many lands,
dust of diaspora in their hems.

Those who know their coming becomes
a poem.
And the old ones, hands as lined and gnarled
as the wailing wall.
Reaching the pinnacle of dream.
Jerusalem,
Jerusalem,
ALIYAH!
ALIYAH!

POEM FOR GREEN SUNDAY

(Green Sunday: project of the Jewish National Fund to plant trees in Israel in honor of family members)

One for our favorite—
the strong-limbed aunt, flamboyant-wigged,
full of lust for life; she of open purse,
of the braided bread, the kitchen of spices.
A lighter of candles, with sparkling hands.
Whose breast was soft,
who would mother the world,
who died in childbirth.

Plant her a fine-limbed tree, so rustled tossing
of leaves perfumes the air.
In whose very twigs nestle these small birds—
their cries and songs,
the flames of their eyes!

And this for the little cousin,
died young. He was so frail
in his heats and fevers,
tossed in his sick-bed, often in pain.
His flesh, desert dry to be dust soon
in the winding-sheet. And Kaddish-sound like
Sirocco winds.
No succulent chicken broth, sesame, no
fragrant tea, or even the Torah
could nourish him on.

Give him a green tree—
with strength he never grew to know.
Let there be humming juices in it.
Let it challenge the hot winds,

shading the parched dry skin of the desert.
Let it grow old.

And a tree for our longest lived—
who had outgrown his need for time
with all its eccentricities,
  but said he would live to be a hundred,
  just to see if God would let him—
  if this is why he had come
  to be—over shaky waters—the hot breath
  of Auschwitz on his neck—
  to his children and children's children
  growing free.
3 days before his hundredth birthday,
turning eyes toward the watery skies
hung above his wallpapered room,
with the chandelier that danced with itself
in his double vision, and
"Your will, God," he said, and died.

3 generations of family; children,
grandchildren, and great-grandchildren
tripled around the bed,
under the circular chandelier,
like the rings of light and dark years.

From barren soil
the bole of his tree will rise up,
branches layered in circular pattern,
out from the great trunk.
The sunlight glitters
a thousand leaves—
as if a huge chandelier hung there
upwards from earth
to swing free in the sky

and be bright for the Lord
three hundred years or more.
"Your will, God."

They will flourish here,
through rings of light and dark years,
they will live on.
The desert will know their names.
Here is where they have their roots.

SALT

No salt like the Gulf of Mexico salt
gull kiss and duck tears in it
    each foamy morning
    hair floating at ebb tide
                scrape   of scale on the skin
from the time of waking up
    the merman's mouth on mine

SENSUAL LANDSCAPE

roads through the valley
                      are mostly orange
smell of orange   and when it rains   the roads
                        are juice, and avocado pulp,
    lemon, sticky   with orange,   sweet
                        sweet orange roads
with juice of honeydew   melons seed spit out
and odor of cantaloupe,
grapefruit smell upon my flesh
flesh becomes avocado   for the mouth   the white
        magnolia between breast and armpit
                clay   soft   the low ruts
    the thirsting root   along long roads
                    breasts heavy as grapefruit
hands grasping fruit firmly
brown field hands   the migrant river's undulation

love has its sensual landscapes the senses revisit

WE SPENT THE NIGHT TOGETHER IN AMSTERDAM

Amsterdam mosquito   who loves my pores
  as Astronauts crave craters of the moon
sending telescopic probes into the milky way
as baby's tongue explores textures of *chocomel*
you suck, balanced on semblance-of-tripod legs,
        my blood.

Sangre de Toro in the gypsy caves of old
                                Madrid
tastes not so sweet (some guitar throb
    will make believe I lie).
But your buzz, many motored thing,
I hear, and see in every multiple moon of eye
    your ecstasy.

Around the corner in the Turkish restaurant—
    that dark-fleshed boy is more erotic treat.
    But you—too lazy to whir there to eat,   or
    you like imports but prefer white meat?

Your forebears got skimped fare across the street
in the great   Poorhouse,
    repository where the indigent,
in social stigma steeped, genteelly starved.
Now it's a convalescent home, and single file,
  a delicacy of almost-dried old skins
  is wheeled each morning to the sun—
you have some virile needs,
    insolent as youth, that
    will not let you taste passivity.
You shun them, like your human prototypes?
                Come here, I'll hit you!
Well, you know, I'd never slay
  even mosquitoes. Peace! You're safe!

Though I love best delirious butterflies
that loll the Flower Market
dripping nectar from their beards,
their hairy bodies, soft antennae, never
hector me—you do!

Say, there's a poet across the next canal
who shares his veins with such exotic stuff
that you'd have visions as you never dreamed,
hallucinate the Giant Archetype
mosquito—
does this interest you?

I fear you haunt the flat plain of this arm,
create a mountainous terrain, only in search
of blood welled in sores' open little pools
on this room's previous occupant
the hospital took off, for leprosy—
a common enough disease here, if you can
understand human talk!—
That old ex-sailor, chest curved like a "c"
who walked across the undulant rug's
thick waves,
daily, past the ship, sails opened wide,
within its windless bottle, going nowhere.

Now under water patterns on the ceiling
sleep, until, in bed,
my body radars its heart's beeps.
You wake to me you've chosen for your feast.
Your urgent bites
leave red marks of your sensuous delight
as souvenirs of Amsterdam
and how we spent this night together.

INTERLUDE IN AN OAKLAND ROSE GARDEN

(a poem-play starring 3 poets identified with Oakland: Gertrude Stein, Rod McKuen, and Jack Kerouac)

Stein: The whorl of the bud
around and around
the vortex in, the pollen down
and around and around and
a stamen thrust and the thorn
unfound
    and around and around
    and the tender bud
found.

McKuen: If you're found
I am your Love-in-June
sit down
        by me
where the bud of your breast
                and the
bloom of the rose so like
lie down   on the ground
by me   where the whorl
in your thighs takes the
pistil thrust

Stein: in and around
and around around
the mouth's petals hold
the pollen found.

Kerouac: And the whorl in the brain
and a vortex found
for the thorn in the vein
when the nectar down
goes in and around

McKuen: and the broken stem
and the song unbound
slips from the mouth
like petal fall

Stein: down and around
the poem the sound
a whorl the sound
and the sound around
and around the sound unwound
and the stem blown of
its hollow of sound
the bud in its pink
in the bloom of the mouth
and the pollen found
and the stamen in
and the pollen found.
The thorn on the stem.
The prick of the thorn.
The pull of the bud,
the petals unbound,
and the fleshy pinks of the
roses found.

Kerouac: But the thrust of thorn at
the heart's vortex
and the pollen into the
whorling mind
and the stamen thrust
that breeds the poem
by the thorn in the prick
and the tear of vein
and the blood unbound
from the fleshy pink
of the bud-shaped heart
when the fleshy petals rip apart

Stein: and the pollen found in the whorl
in the bud around and around.

BLOOD ROSE BOUQUET

Where the ice of Cleaver's soul
becomes a diamond in the sky
a blood-red rose frozen within it
solidified in space
to circle forever
centering the black holes
refracting light rays
of moon and sun
(for we also lose direction look for light
turn and turn) for the lonely space traveler.

And Patty Hearst's white face looks out
the narrow bars of the Oakland jail
one more little cell in the cellular link
of us all in our terrible inhumanity.

Bobby Seale & Gertrude Stein and
Robert Louis Stevenson & Mary Rudge
and Maya Angelou
hold hands and dance in the widening circle
of spirits in the heavens over Oakland
for Oakland is a Holy City

and in the palms of a 13 year old
    black Oakland girl
    the stigmata have appeared.

SOON THE CITY WILL BURST INTO SONG

(for Charles Shere)

Soon the city will burst into song.
The movies show us how to do it.
We learn everything from movies.
Twenty-three thousand people attended
  the musical today.

First, a secretary steps outside the
  door of her office and sings.
She is wearing a long pastel pink dress.
Every secretary in every other
  identical office cubicle comes out.
They all know the same song, their dresses
  are long   pastel pink or yellow.

The City Center is filled with cooing doves.
  Young men in sailor suits wait for buses
  under the new trees—but they are moved
    to dance instead.
  They slide over cement that has sparkles in it.
  Somehow they love these secretaries.
  By now appear clerks in slim flannel suits;
    and women pulling children,
    humming snatches of song—
    hurrying by.
  The employers of all these singing secretaries
    are male. They wear dark blue,
    and maroon ties.
    They arrive for the finale.

Pale and intense, a bearded man
composes secret sonatas,
on the fourth floor of that building,
past editorial desks,
hears electronic music on the typewriter keys.

Arias of La Traviata and La Boheme
   seem to echo
   up elevator shafts,
   and on the lips of tenor boys saying, "Copy."

A Broadway has shown all Broadways how to sing.
   The lighting gets mysteriously blue,
   Porgy rolls round a corner his low cart—
   Mack the Knife, followed by chorus of girls in
   slit short satin, goes into his act.
There's dancing and singing in the streets today!
Two patrol cars stage a shootout only so a hero of
   West Side Story persuasion
   can do a jazz-rock number
         from curb to curb!

Jesus Christ Superstar is playing a corner church.
Folk Guitar Masses resound against storefronts.
   The streets are absolutely deserted,
         it's Sunday noon.
   Someone in levis and boots
is striding right down the center of the street
         singing a lone lament
         very close to the sunset.

CABLE CAR, I AM THE SCRIBE OF LOVE

Cable Car, I am the Scribe of Love

and these vibrations in the rails
these whirling wheels have
set my pen   spinning
up and down the page.

  This is not for difficult people filled with doubts
  but for the easy brave with believable destiny;
all of us will arrive safe and soon,
    mouths sweet and moist with mists,
The gripman moves us on by a
        muscular twist to a shaft
and the ambience shifts in the wake of streets
with an overlapping history.

The bell in musical ballad tells;
here Stanford and Muybridge
    invented motion pictures,
here Phineas T. Farnsworth developed television,
here time moves fast, and images change!
Here is a moving collage
of our lives.
Flowery stars are loose in our hands,
petals hold in lapels,
the tail of the dragon kite trails the air,
as we open our gestures upon the hills,
eyes flicker past swift scenes
thick with textures.
  Here we are held but an instant
  above cadmium red,
  above greens—veridian,
  and the blue-green-blue of Bay
  water that ripples and rocks in changing light

all the way to Tiburon—
gulls sensing their flight through grey fog.

We hang close to the hill
by tenacity of cable roiled on
its strong wheel.
It is a form of simple courage—
this great swoop up
and over—
this ride—
and I am the Scribe of Love who writes it down.

ARRIVAL POEM

The bus comes
      breathing its inner fire
      becomes green dragon.
We've entered the shared theme
   of unknown destinies
            holding poems whose endings we
                  mean to rewrite.

At one with Mary Shelley; for these seats
of dinosaur and other hides are stitched
in seams designed by Dr. Frankenstein.

At one with Poe; balanced precariously over
sewer veins tunneling intricately under the
city their horrific mysteries.

We are Huck Finns, on frail raft
running rapids through rock and alligator gar
(we know what allegory *they* are).

We beam
upon each other   talking to strangers
in holy consummation of our journeying

transfers—confetti of the celebration
of commuting—fall in my daydreams.

NO EATING—RADIOS SILENT: A SIGN

On this bus
sneaking the last
of the Milky Way
We did not share
YOU SHALL NOT EAT
We don't find out who
died in hunger
turn off news—

This is no freedom ride
for cause
RADIOS SILENT

Someone has doubled their fist over
a fare   or a transfer
expired

YOU SHALL NOT EAT
others chew
in embarrassed isolation
look away   quiet   silent   silent

suspended in a special atmosphere
(like formaldehyde)
where we don't have to
feel or fear
only ride
from here to there
inanimate   for all we care
YOU SHALL NOT HUNGER
WE SHALL NOT HEAR

WITH HEAVENLY DISPATCH

Rosa Parks rerouted the direction
of history from a bus seat

Let me feel Ezekhiel's big wheel & little wheel
in my hand

There are people on this bus
who hate each other

still

People sitting in the middle who do not
understand.

GETTING OFF

As lumbering slow
as hundred year old tortoise
slips along in its shell, its side scraping,
the heavy thump and drag of a great foot,
coral shadows cast on our faces.
  I feel a press against a density of space
and underwater currents jerk us to their flow.
  There is a gaunt and cavern-eyed
  old man behind me
  he shakes the bus with shudders of his crying.
  Like Jonah, he is hunched in dreadful destiny,
  and in this hollow belly
  racked by an uttered pain,
  but going—beyond his own strength—
  going on.
These passengers, rigid, erect, as bone ribs
  in their spaces,
  have placed stones in their ears
  against sirens, so hear no sorrow;
  having paid already parts of their hearts
  as token of having touched sea bottom.
  Some wear shark's tooth
  embedded as a sign. Their breasts are sand-bars.
  They are searching secret wave lengths
  for their eyes. A far-off sound, as of a ship's bell,
  signals safe passage through rocks
    and shoals, for whom—for whom—
An albatross has pressed its heavy weight
against my window,
I will wrench my shoulder free.
I'll get off at the next island—
running through feathers—running through
    rip-tide—
and nothing, when I go, can ever catch me!

COMMUTE

Commuters in their sand colored shirts
their cowhide colored suits
their tanned leather colored suits
their boots polished to bronze
their saddle soaped leather brief cases
their skin browned to rawhide
their horseshoe shaped belt buckles
        gleaming semi-circles
            across low bulge of bellies
the bulge of the crotch
            like leather bags
the beginning of pouches
            below the eyes
(the wrinkled-leatherfolds at eye edge—
    sun-wrinkle, vertical between the brows)
        that see the tributaries of rivers
            coiled as a mess of rattlesnakes
the one long two-lane road unrolled
                thick and loose its lariat
the 4-lane freeway that flowers into eight
                wide lanes at the cloverleaf
by a Stetson-big basin of water
            surrounded with pine fringe
the   straw curled-brim hat   on knee's bend
the hand fumbling the 14-karat gold pen
the notebook folded back
            a trail herd of fat black cadillacs.
                Corralled by concrete.

After all that passed of scrimping for cause
acres of bottomland to give to a son
and a 2-story, clapboard house and grove of
            pecan trees down a gravel road
            and its own deep well.

THE ROCKS OF FOLSOM PRISON

Rock quarry
looming
the rocks of Folsom Prison embed you to
        one spot on earth.
Going free over mountains
I walk the rim road of mountains to you.
Rockfalls moved by my foot's path to you
      roll resound like bones
      fall long below treetops.
Death is a depth, a dry brittle rolling,
      a fall of stone.
In love I walk the rimroad of mountain
        toward you.
  In mountains are tunnels ratruns ores roots
  alluvial movements of seed and rocks
  under the rocks of Folsom Prison.
    Lying awake crushed under rockslide
      to wonder if
    there is rescue has a search gone out
    your sex is imprisoned
    your balls are a petrified rock
    your gonads rock hard
    your seed brittle and dried
stoned by rock and when a dawn,
        like granite, breaks
assigned to break rock
for those who come after you.
There are guns focused on you to make
you break open rocks
I tell you—knowing all the time that when
sons ask for bread we do not give
give them stones.

CO-EXISTING

("To him everything is food except granite." John Muir of the grizzly.)

Thin membrane of tent holds us
in mountain meadow, hours between
        dark and light
to sleep. Under our shoulder-blades press
tubers, roots, bears' food.
Our hands move on the mounds where seeds,
developing below ground, vulnerable
        as little breasts,
shudder and tremble as they swell from within.
Ear against earth, we wake to hear
movements through meadow grass
that make us know our own
fleshy smell is meat.

Our teeth as bears' teeth, took
those bitter berries bitten in the sun,
whose shell still spreads a tartness on the tongue.
We cooked the rabbit at the campfire, ate,
then, leaped and swam, curving as fish, upstream.
      Water slid, sparkling, from the
  bear's fur, his paw scooped the silver fish,
  arcing through sun. The bear
  ambles on rodent path
  and rabbit run in meadow grass.
  Flesh of the rabbit quivers. Membrane of
    skin torn.

IMMIGRADOS

The paregoric   simply seemed better
      in the cup glazed
purple. Somehow she always had to have it—
eyeless worms, amoebas, lime-green eels
spawned in the intestines at night.
      Dreadful things
continued to happen. The top of the water jug
constantly fell in the toilet.
She would go into the jungles of   San Blas
her mouth full of blisters.
Unable to learn the language she couldn't
really communicate.
Accumulating dreams we continued painting,
composing music for reed pipes easily found.
We knew we would never
grow old breaking our veins on cement,
building civilization's abominations.
She kept a parrot,
and a glazed purple cup for the paregoric.

STRANGER AT THE OPEN MARKET

Under the star-apple tree,
the boy in the sari-sari store,
sells young coconut halves,
to girls with Chinese eyes,
and Spanish names,
who mix Tagalog with other tongues.
Graceful the dance of their arms,
in butterfly sleeves'
embroidered pineapple fibers.
The barefoot poor wear sha-sha-sha sound
of banana leaves.
Men with beauty tattoos.
What do I do, bizarre foreigner,
at this Bazaar
of others' lives?
Shop for one turn of phrase,
some laugh's description?
Finger a palm bark texture
where my mind has printed a word?
Stuffing my mouth with melons
and sentences fall like spit seeds.

(Written in collaboration with Amy Estrada.)

Sari-sari store: small variety store.

NOW ME

The snake bone
that protects against lightening
great grandmother wore
great grandfather bought
for one goat and two ducks more.
    Their son—grandfather—went
    to harvest American crops.
    Money and letters stopped.
    No one heard again.

Grandmother bore
the child alone
    and watched these waters
        wondering
        what was sure
        in the ebb and flow
            below
wharves piled with hemp rope
baled for the holds of ships
leaving the Archipelagos
low on seas thick with squid
    and pompano.
Sea that showed image of her own eyes,
tears on the medal
    of Fatima.

My mother, long way from the barangay.
My father in his crocodile skin shoes.
  Lovers riding the caramata,
  sharing halo-halo in the botica,
  kissing, under the mangroves
  marked with Spanish sabre slashes,
wore rings with the seal of their school
and class year—sure, without charm or spell,
skill and love alone, would serve them well.

Now, me. Leading this carabao,
   among the narra trees,
in these thousands-unnamed islands.
Feel, underfoot, dried backbone of the snake,
near the medal fallen through banana leaves,
where the classrings rust in compost
by the gravestone.

I, too, will be tossed and winnowed,
against some winds of chance,
and elements that bring
            the lightning.

(Written in collaboration with Amy Estrada.)

Caramata: horse-drawn cart.
Halo-halo: mixed fruits topped with crushed ice
   and milk.
Botica: drugstore with snack area.
Carabao: water buffalo.

GANYAN ANG BUHAY NATIN
(THAT IS THE WAY LIFE IS)

In the wild grass
    in the yard
  we collect grasshoppers
    dragonflies.
Sometimes we keep them
in small bamboo cages.
Small things which live
  we hold—and they die—
  ganyan ang buhay natin
  (that is the way life is).

    There is a long walk to the river.
    There are dead dogs in the river.
Makakaraos din.
(Somehow we'll manage.)

People eat the kang kong
(waterlily vegetation)
that grows in the water.
Every time there is a flood
all this dead dog dirty water
comes up to the thighs
  of us in the city.
It's so brown. The brown children swim
      in the streets.
We walk into this house still in the water
breeding place for mosquitoes
        and more living things,
up on ladder-stairs to sleep.

This bamboo will hold for a long time.

Makakaraos din.
(Somehow we'll manage.)
Ganyan ang buhay natin.
(That is the way life is.)

(Written in collaboration with Amy Estrada.)

GRAVEWARD TO IRELAND

(. . . as no men to carry it are left, his coffin is carried by women . . .)

Sisters, with the weight of his flesh
and bones on the bones of our shoulders,
in this box that holds,
as we hold it, our brother
set toward that decay
thick with waiting worms, how we
women who would carry men in the womb,
and on the quick bare length
of our limbs in wedlock,
we whose vows to love men
are never carried lightly,
heavily, we, the barren, bear the beloved of
sterile death
as the pall, blood, sinew,
bones like stones, and heavy heart,
of all war-bearing men—
our old dad, see his photo
framed in bog oak,
and his father, *his* father's father
whose curls still flicker red gold
in a circlet of tatting we were each
to carry to the marriage Mass as
something old, old—
hold collective angers and guilts of
ancestors.
Those ancients discovering peat fire,
asleep in the open,
before crude hands
learned to pack sod huts,
back, even to Noah, his first drunk dream ashore
disturbed by lusts carried in the Ark,
back, back, to the common father of all men,
Adam, his son a brother's murderer,

  as we carry in our genes their cells,
and on our back, who died for religion's
relics and ritual, "do good for evil,"
commandment never understood;
        "thou shalt not kill."
Saying The Sorrowful Mysteries,
as the celibates tell us
how to love men,
now the splinters from burial's
coarse wood covering
pierce our skin
as we shoulder the last corpse—
                    no men left for us,
                    no men here.

Who will love us, sisters, who will we love?
The long dead brothers of the girl who
will never bear our brother's children?
They are weightless ghosts at our side,
and the word has come to us
over blood-wet clover,
     electric through air
     and in letters of tearblack ink,
     that the women in every county
     cry too, for dead men,
     cry there,
        that the Protestants are crying,
                    sisters,
        Protestant sisters cry now
        "there are no more men—
no men
none   none   none."
And we will be   chaste nuns
of religion, for faith they died amen   for a land
where women   grievously weeping graveward
have borne the men.

FOR WOMEN IN FRINGED SHAWLS

(for Natica who choreographed this poem)

Knowing, with shawl's
fringe sweeping the floor
how many years women have been
    sweepers of this world.
Twigs tied on stick   brush—brush
the dirt that boys track in.
    Sweep—sweep the crumbs the men leave.

I am proud to sweep this hall
    with these long fringes of my shawl.
I am the woman poet and   sweep before me
        all women up
        to the podium,
  flutter and   brush the air, this fringe.
I know the fringes of men's world
where old poems sent women
        to sweep the sky
    with witch-screech, screaming
          from brooms,
  to tell darkness their dreams.
They would sweep the moon;
Astronauts leave garbage for them there,
still,
debris of mankind   circling in place.

"You have an instinct for this broom,"
they said, and read how Cinderella swept,
right off his feet, a prince;
discovery to inspire sweeping all space!
"Cleanliness is next to Godliness,"
I heard on Sunday.
God's kingdom   as the prince's   comes to me
for my pure industry. Sweep-sweep the room.

Broom, existential tool,
for woman's primal work—would keep the earth.
  Sweep dead bats from cave.
Her territory was the hearth; inheritance,
            ash.

Who would believe Imaginary world
  where women sweep out Princes, yes
  those politicians, toads,
    who let the babies starve
    and children sleep in streets
    flies on filth of their faces!
I, wrapped in this symbolic shawl
        with long fringe sweeping
    stride to the microphones and call
      on men in unswept
white house, castle, kremlin, pentagon, you who
unfurl flags over your wars' array-for-murder—
      some big mess to sweep up
now you weep in secret how death's angel's
feather-fringed wings fold on all men—

"See," I say, "women with fingers, fringes, palms,
  ready around to hold you to life!"

I sweep the floor,
the air, clear for this vision—
until you feel, in the winds, fringe
brush your face, your room, your world.

So, so, in this fringed shawl I,
    you would send to sweep,
    have come to sweep
    the cobwebs from the skies
    your eyes.

A BLESSING FOR WOMEN

bless all of the women carrying
plastic shopping bags
full of plastic flowers
and bless the women holding paper sacks
of celery, collard greens, day-old bread
and hard edge cans
and bless all mothers waiting in lines
in food stamp offices or day care centers
filling out forms in triplicate
in pink & white & ochre papers papers papers
listing for the 12th time each child
date of birth and mother's mother's
maiden name and father's whereabouts
unknown or even father unknown
bless all of the women carrying babies
on buses walking carrying babies
babies that overpopulate that grow to go to
juvenile hall or mental clinics
that are later scarred by acne
hearts like pits pared of fruit
bless all the women in the
grocery store who
read and wonder
letting roll over the tongue the
sound of beautiful names of teas
lemon verbena yerba buena dragonwell
lavender who read them as a poem
who would cure you with their soups
who try to tell their love

IN THE WOMEN'S ROOM

I

In the northwest rooms of an old
victorian madhouse
where nothing is in context
the aspidistra is a metal sculpture
cast iron andirons holding paper fires
light   prisms in cut-glass   and
translucence of wax flowers
we are a wax museum, or walls of
      portraits in oils   where past inexplicable
blends into the anew
I live out women's guess-works and unconditions.

II

Persia, Bangladesh,
   and South of France share hungers
   on my pillows   eating oranges
   under wind chime chandeliers
   that cast spectrums of interchangeable
                  colors
   of joys and fears in rainbow unity
                        across our eyes
   music boxes are our hearts
   against the children's ears.

III

Modigliani odalisque   upon the rug
water-lily head on tube of neck
   dragonfly eyes, water patterns
   of that wild and flowing hair

ripples and whirlpools and waterfalls in it.
Yes, waters' rapids laugh against your teeth
small pebbles
and your hands water striders
on the green moss algae rug.

IV

and water   flawed by becoming a fleshy   being
and grass and flowers   tapestry without
a warp and weft of fragrance.
The bird in its cage turns its heart into a seed
tendril in midair.
In clockwork recall the history of
other women's lives ticks in the bookcase
life's throb pressed
and bound forever.

O CHILDREN, MOTHER WANTED TO BE A POET!

Did I never eat breadfruit,
research the Samoan sexrite,
dust archeological digs
toward the perilous curvature of
the dinosaur egg?
Patiently, patiently, I stand
in the doubleburger line
at McDonalds, the center of a cyclone in my eye.
Exiled, estranged in Supermarkets,
have you seen me lately,
Children?
I lost my mind around 6th Street,
where I would meet myself
coming and going;
there is a corner lightpost,
a succulent in that garden whose name I knew.
I have remembered to pay for the daily news,
carrier of my obituary.
I have been in this Ford for days,
in this Nursery Co-op
years. When the parents meet,
my feet go to sleep in
old shoes, while the wild horse in me
breaks the reins,
galloping, galloping, be a poet, be a poet.
Even as I draw designs, on the fragile
curvature of the
Easter egg, daughters
with breasts described by Old Testaments
remember. I wanted to be,
before Day Star, BE, be a poet.
Research the Samoan sexrite.
Eat breadfruit. Follow the
sound of the word around

the perilous curvature of the skull.
O Children. O yes remember, Children.
Mother wanted to be
(patiently I stand in line), a poet.

Children, I have taken you to the zoo,
the California bear dancing
for passing ladies, the people with
Saturday off, to feed the untamed lion
in my hunger, hear
the orang-ou-tan rattle the chainswing
against the cage bar,
picking up peanut shells my audience
throws. See
the primal element in the lemur's eyes.
Confined to my grotto, saying rosaries
for First Communions,
for poets in Argentina, in Poland, in Roumania,
arrested by the junta, the coup,
the changing of times—
cell-bar shadows
on their faces.
In this Ford, this nursery school co-op,
the junta of time, in Love's coup,
with the cell-bar shadows
of your fingers on my face
across the fragile curvature of my skull, never
eating breadfruit, researching
the Samoan sexrite,
digging toward perilous curvature of earth's
fragile egg,
Children, O YES Children, O yes
REMEMBER Children,
Mother wanted to be a poet!

THREAD OF WOMAN SEWING
(a poem play for 6 voices)

Voice 1

Now in my hand continuous thread
   outlining multicolored vision
   of these women—
ancestors, and sisters,   binding
                              together
   tight knots of families,
   tangled strands of race—
taut leather thongs of women
that   breathe hot sand
women whose feet leave thin red
   threads of blood on the
   knives of rock
women whose laugh refutes fear,
   uncurling like ribbons in air,
old women, unraveling strands
   still they tie
   to worn traditions
   uncompleted generations,
past to future, country to
country, stitched and pieced.

Voice 2

I didn't ask mom—just came home after
and said, "It's done, I've enlisted."
She had that strained look that I
didn't want to see.
She told me, "You've broken the thread!"
I was the first to leave the family.

Voice 3

The two years before she died my
mother's mother
withdrew to her own room to sew
Sometimes she had the light on far into
the night. It seems she didn't sleep,
keeping her fingers fast around the shapes
of cloth. Sewn keepsakes. "For you," she said,
"your cousins, sisters, each one. In that
cedar chest your heritage from me . . . "
handstitched, embroidered. All those nights
and days,
I saw her through the not-quite-shut door,
outlined over linen vague in darkness,
the radio turned very low—once, Beethoven,
and she murmured, "he was deaf." I realized
that she was really nearly blind, sewing a
design she couldn't see,
through dark.
When she was dying I wondered,
sitting by the bed, "Gran,
you didn't go to church, never asked, but is
there anyone besides the family you want
to be with you—somebody to talk to who is—
well—religious?"
But she answered, "Design that
I cannot see—I know it."

Voice 4

I grew old young. We lived in a housing project other people called "The Boxcars"—8 families in each structure, no fire escapes, paper thin walls. In three families of my building there was suicide. Most were on welfare. The man downstairs bed-ridden, spine curled like an embryo. When flames sparked from the tattered wiring, one of his young children locked the door to his bedroom," so the fire couldn't get daddy"—then they ran out. The building was—gone—in 20 minutes, before the firemen came. Everyone was crying just as if they were all the same race! Just that morning women called each other dago, nigger, spick, & wop! Brawling over the clothesline spaces, invoking ancient curses from their separate races—crying now together as one voice, one stitched-by-suffering face.

Voice 5

Her kitchen was awash with moving color
come through a prism
          swaying from a string
               refracting rainbows' lights
by day—
                    at night
she moved swung by the fragile thread
                              of sleep
     through swirling technicolor of her dreams.

Voice 6

Her song came out from her across water
like the fragrance of flowers from land
          floating
          rippling
when the oar dipped.

"Oh, I love you, I love you!" she was
     calling. Even before
the circle of rope slipped
over the moorhead

her arms twined tight at my neck,
and we lost our footing, and fell, laughing,
splashing water, her wet skirt
billowed out, and, our feet swirling,
we pulled each other over into the boat,
our bodies rocking it up against the dock
with hard and thudding rhythms   of our love.

Voice 1

We are conceived, with the cord that feeds us,
        in the bodies of strong women.
There is a connecting thread between us all—
        reality and dream and memory.
Now in my hand, outlining multicolored vision
          of ancestors and sisters,
   strong women,   this continuous thread.

QUILT PIECE

The deep south ladies are driving their cream
colored Cadillacs and Continentals through
afternoon shade of the long-needle pines.
Those stiff straight trees have held up this small
town sky for centuries. Light and dark intensify
a pattern over   unchanging years, falling on
plush bed of road,   needles, and cones.
You cannot see sky from beneath these pines.
The sun cannot change these pale southern ladies.
    They play bridge in long low living rooms
    among bric-a-brac several ancestors old,
    genteelly their china cups clink in the saucers,
    laying the cards in ritual patterns,
    eating the layers of late summer strawberries
    on lush cream. The air conditioner metallically
    clicks. The grandfather clock measures
    their long conversations.
They compare with a sadness behind slow voices,
  the cancers' progress within their bodies,
  the arthritis creeping that curls their bones.
  Talking of old Miz Bess who's laid in her
        room now
  eighteen years and is more than eighty,
        with the
  shades down, staying alive on little bitty sips
  of tea, they say, oh, and occasional slivers
  of chicken breast. And one will sigh,
  and go into the kitchen, and with her
        own hands
dip off a little pot likker from the evening's roast
  for the apricot poodle whose dish is set
  in the same spot on the old veranda
  where the blue hound's bowl would stay.
These ladies, as the shadows deepen
        between the trees,

gather their stoles that glisten as if, still,
        small mink
and ermine quiver the fur, turning the cold air up
in the cars, to justify the living feel
of pelts at their shoulders and folds of chins,
the stars of their diamonds keep practiced orbit
on the steering wheels.
                Under the roads lie the same
ruts their grandmothers' wagons creaked
        through,
over a hundred years before—
below these pines that
seem to be needles of the universe, stitching
        together
the world they know—
        coming home from the quilting bee.

STRANGE GIRL

Alligator gar in the Sabine River.
Swinging bridge across the Sabine River.
Curve your body out from the cable-strung side
see up through the dust the fireflies thick
to the starry skies in endless dancing
and sun motes days in the dry dust swirl
up through the heat-bronzed thickness of trees
down
to blue green long slick slow
curving river below
that tallest massive tree
where the burnt-short rope end sways in the
gentle wind
where the hanged man
swung out over the water
black? white? that didn't matter
to the hooded men
massed thick on
the bridge
hung over the siderope
pressed against it
swung with their weight
creaked separate
boards
against the span-ropes
lynched the town drunk less than human
slept on
the street like a dog old-trembly
in the way
hadn't no family
said he took bread
out of the gen'ral store
made an example of him—staggering fool—
whispered it around so the young'uns knew

too big for lickens
too big for their britches
bootleg cars jacked up and weighted
with rocks so the trunk hung level
going over dry and coming back wet
cross the border
with rot-gut 'stead of rocks   be a lesson—
the man hung over the somber river
seething with gar-fish
firefall of sparks gushing up and up
while he burned until the rope
burned
through and he spun and splashed
fierily into the Sabine River   that great
sizzle of water on flame   until the
gar gnashed all the remains of the
charred mass
so my pop said
alcohol burns with a blue flame
said the eyes burned long in the
hollow
sockets of the skull bone
in dark water
We boys was gigging frogs
the croaking scream
as the gig goes in
in the night when the light hits
frog legs jerk in the skillet like living-leaping
when the hot
grease gits them
flame from long-needle pine was crackling
we
was passing a
jug of red-eye,
you new here   you,
strange girl,   got to learn our ways
to get along,
just let your head lean back out

over the river that
long hair float in air look up there
past the
rope end through the trees
up on the ridge   see
there she lives
tied her by her thick braids to the tree trunk
six of us
give it to her   quick like the frog gig
blood and   the screams   until—
we thought her dad would take his rifle
when he heard   his
fury flared once in the eyes set deep
in the half-coyote face and flicked out
to a laugh half-snort half-snarl
said guess as how   she was going to get it
one way or another   sooner or later
don't hold no grudge
in the backwoods—
jes high-spirited boys—see
ain't like a city   where no one knows
a neighbor's business—next spring
her pa married her to that puny old miser
over
Razorback Hog Bend
buried one child died young in the
north forty of his farm,   ain't been
the same since
when her pa's trees burned they said she done it
no one seen such flames   shoot up the night
you heard of them volcanos
fright like that   alright
red flowed down over everything
rich charred pulp it smoked days
those embers like the crusts of hell
big timber flared and fell
come glowing streams through sky
into the Sabine River

where the gar turned belly-up
sights we've seen
deep woods all ingrown
to each other,
strange girl,   I got to say
you don't understand our ways
you won't be happy here.

MOON GAME

Earth was our childhood toy,
the rearrangeable rocks and animal bones.
Feathers multicolored for gathering.
Earth's parts held. Good to the hand.
  Palm cupped on press of warm egg's shell.
Intricate movement of whittling knife
    skillfully worked against wood.
  The finger fit in the trigger's curve
    of the double-barrelled gun.
  Animals—flexing their muscles
    under our touch—that moaned
    and died of their lesser years.
  How sinews' pull, in the body's swing
    with axe or hoe, could thrill.

Still, we feared the invisible hand
that moves the planets.
Fissures opened in fields that betrayed
          our trust.
Varmints unseen, haunting the mind,
    crawled through our dreams.
Those ring-tailed terrors, the wall-eyed cojo
    elusive as snipe.
Death ever-ready to take us with fangs
        of cottonmouth snake.

Here   we've walled them out! Do others crave
  an untouchable   Space?
We   have games secure in the hold of our hand.
Let old wives yammer and murmur their tales—
    how dogs revert to wild and devour
        their masters,
    cats suck breath in the night,
    boys lust after beasts; mares, calves,
      no female creature escapes their sex—

of the bonfire in women,
some days of their stars
sullen, dripping blood.

All walled-out. We have built a hall
for our games that gleam in the yellow light—
men among men—
balls racked for our cues. Dominoes. Cards.
Let the moon game go on all night.
Again tomorrow. Last forever.

(Unacknowledged rites of initiation into Southern manhood included being admitted into Moon Parlors, and Billiard Parlors where pool, dominoes, card and moon games are played. Women and children were never allowed, but could stand out on the sidewalk—dirt, or boards in some sections of town—and look in, to deliver a message or try to get their men to come home. Women could play cards or dominoes at home. Richer, more educated women had bridge parties. I do not know any women who learned the moon game. I felt this had its parallel with the first male-only astronauts going to the moon.)

GOAT FARM

Goatherd, grave-eyed girl
3 acres through a eucalyptus grove
goes close with her small group
of smooth-haired split-foot sisters,
gathers some to their stalls
some, full, for milking.
Sweet molasses,
and alfalfa's pungent layers ripening
the shed.
Among the bred
brood-does,
year after year remembering,
lured and repelled
the buck, his virile smell!
She's seen each spring
some pregnant females
fill until
small bodies grown round to a
groaning point
bulge into tender hands
their birth—
and she virgin, against realities
of seasons,
lured and repelled
recalls the buck's
strong smell. Eyes on swollen bellies
of the does, murmuring
among the bleating in the shed
her sisterhood.
"You, I love and care for."
"You," she promises across the yarrow field,
"You," to the close group
in the eucalyptus grove.

SLEEK HEAD PLEASING YOURSELF

Before you command its cutting
I fill my heart with not forgetting
the way your hair looked
when it grew long—
long as thousand small grasses
and wild flowers of Mt. Bruno
full of dust and summer—
as waves of Bay waters,
flow of the the Estuary,
in the wake of your going,
pale new tendrils on treetops
on Mt. Tamalpais.
Faun-eyes-memories
and wood smoke wisps and snowy owl wing
        feathers   when your hair fluttered
            in its own winds.

When you decide it is a burden
held on a slender frame,
a nuisance to brush out electric sparks,
and you're irritable and maddened by its
sunflower blaze on your neck's slight stalk
I'll never blame you.

If it falls to be swept on the floor,
    coiled in a drawer,
    sold,
in my heart's eye I'll see it, scattered
    in meadow of fern and leaves—
tangled with weed   rooted
    touched earth   to me it will be the
        wild   ponies tail
    of dusky scrub horse   sought by ropes of
        civilization.
    You will be

as the snake in his new skin slipped from
his past.
I will see you lamb sheared, sleek head
pleasing yourself
and all that hair   that wild hair   loosed
will brush forever past my lips   fragrant
with wreaths of berries, tousled clover
and small sweet flowers.

NEW ICARUS

Finding feathers on the rocks I glue them
        along lines of these poems
        making them winged.
Folding poems into kites on the beach I
        let them fly.
I walk the tide-line, seeing
    in every half shell and fragment, juices of
    sea urchin, and bay brine.
I drink. I crack open clams' locks and eat.
Here the sand bank has fallen away and
    roots hang in space, below the ledge
    that holds still living beachgrass.
Driftwood has inscribed its pattern
    on the whorl of my fingerprint.

Here I am marooned on an island with a book.
    Flotsam of a fast world going down
    slowly into airy seas—
    in the galaxy's infinite formation,
    one star vessel no longer seaworthy.

Icarus, my earth,
tendrils suspended in space hang there
one more moment,
life-support disintegrating, while I wing
myself in poems for that abandonment,
uncharted shipwreck into space,
taking all of your imprint on my cells, my seed.

THE DREAM—KING (MARTIN LUTHER KING)

The vision yes the dream exists
and men are born to it
in kaleidoscopic-color-pattern beauty
over earth and time. The pieces in the
grand design
have names like Gandhi, Chavez, King,
Mother Teresa, Dorothy Day—
and more. Let future fragment come—turn,
kaleidoscopic turn,
for small child born next door
or this one in your arms.
Does first the man exist
and then the dream?
Some rare and complex
cellular connection certainty
compels one into destiny?
How was it for all of them? Turn,
kaleidoscopic turn.
How was it with King?
The dream for the man, the man for
the dream,
that he could not be overcome
the dream is overcoming all.

King said, "Come rise up marching strong to Washington to right the wrong that prejudice to birth or skin does to all men." The students came and movie stars and simple people near and far. Said King, "When I looked around me and saw the faces of every age and from all the races—how they came by groups like SNICK and CORE and they kept on coming more and more and *overcoming* was what it was for." Said King, "In my heart I had to see how I could love them all for they came from so long in time to be in this long march with me—for they loved me—and it was Love would see Justice done and I could not be overcome, this love would overcome."

The millions watching on TV
saw him at the balcony,
heard the bullet-zing with its bloodred sound
and the thud of the body in pain
brought down—
heard the mourners in church
singing with one voice
"Amazing Grace"—
how *well* King had made his choice
to go in peace even to death
and the passionate breast quiet of
his breath.
So could he have *lived*, quiet, safe, serene,
and the *dream* never been—
But he knew that once he had begun
he would never be overcome
and his peace flows out to the world beyond
Overcoming all—

At peace with everlasting Life
and he shall not be overcome—
this dream is overcoming all.

As the kaleidoscope turns
for the next man's dream
or the dream's next man—
and turns again—
so the clear light burns
as a stained-glass window
of the place
that refracted colors of King's face
for history's eternity.

Turn kaleidoscopic turn
where names like Gandhi, Chavez,
Mother Teresa,
Turn
kaleidoscopic turn.
Pieces in the grand design
change and move. Reality—
the dream exists
the vision
Yes!

PAUL MCCARTNEY: APOCALYPSE IN VENICE

(News item: " . . . former Beatle . . . raised $75,000 in a UNESCO rock concert in Venice . . . to save that picturesque and historic city . . . steadily decaying through . . . tides and pollution.")

Pull Venice up on a high note.
Balance it precariously   on a tremulo.
Sea sirens pull in counterpoint,
Venice, whose foundations slow erode, and
sand by sand crumble into cracks, into corals.
Venice, sinking down in vertical light
to cool green grottos where naiads
and mermen flip their long tails
over balconies, laugh,
lying on their backs in canopied beds,
below currents   that drag wet draperies
through the tides; staring in glee at ceilings
where light distorts
                    in crustacean chandeliers,   see,
from roofbeams,
barnacles suck the water's sweets.
        Pinnacle towers of cathedrals
        hold bells whose calls
        echo where shells' spirals
        flute their openings,
calling the drowned to celebrate at the side altars
        no further seasons
        no rain.
Shapes of sharks grope clumsily   under the pews.
            Alto and soprano fuse with a sobbing lost
                    below wavecrash!

            There is a chorus (repeat)
            Atlantis sank
            and no one was singing.

Who could save Venice
with green foundation of money
blending to seagreen,
silver coins to catch in skeletons of
starfish,
or far, far up dark cool currents over
sunken steeple
lonely gondolas
float with no rider
no place of embarkment?
Only song can save her,
Venice sinking.
Through cosmos charged by
lengths and waves
of sound bringing
transition,
sing—
and music stirs the atmosphere—
note-combinations click the molecules
changing the atoms in their dance
so waters only kiss the people gently—
and set the city free to laugh on air.

PLANTING A REDWOOD FOR ROBINSON JEFFERS

(planted in 1980 by William Everson and California Writers at Joaquin Miller park in Oakland)

Here the thunderhead
   has reared its profile over the Bay
      in the hills of Oakland
         a torrent of breath.
Jeffers' maelstrom
   on Everson's tongue. In
mounting tides of afternoon
   flooding the city where a
      catholic sea left separate starfish
adrift near the Mormons' temple
awash at old St. Albert's priory,
tidepools of the generous Pacific,
      every deep wave-heave will mix them.
Here   each dawn
   Jehovah gathers, multi-colored,
      people like shells into the hand.
Here, where Juanita Miller, the white witch,
   guarded bleached whalebones
      of her father.
      At the fire circle   images crackle.
      Syllables crest, and ripple out
      to islets of listeners.
Boat by boat, old sailors, we will cast nets wide
            for words,
dive, crack oysters, barnacles, in the breakers,
   take   clams from muds by bucketfuls,
         wave after wave awash with poets.
Grasping each other from death by slow drowning
in Atlantis we built ourselves
      float,
      collecting the undertow's treasures
            with waterlogged fingers,

for posterity transcribing
on driftwood   lifelines of our palms.
Remember how hand to hand
we gave souvenirs of books
in the tradewinds,
on land of drifted sands on the backs
of turtles that slumber and wake
and slumber again for our sake.
Remember how the hair's cirrus clouds—
the hair's foams—dissolve in
rising mists,
then and tomorrow.
The seahawks
disappeared
will you remember us?
Fluid, the poem
escapes the net.
"He wanted no disciple,"
Everson said.
We throw the nets
on Jeffers' granite sea.

Here where our tears for the
hard land he wrote dry,
the empty shell's concentric
opens to heaven,
floodtides have
lathered these grasses
and seeped in the ground,
the living redwood rooted
grasps wet earth, we
set its destiny—
into the centuries.

READING THE POEMS

And dropping his backpack to the floor—
the books in it clunking
    sounds bronze as old bells and as
    the thung of the carpenter's tools on
          new doorframes—
the poet
          stepped to the podium—
          said now I build—this room
    was full of vibrations.
    Strange wild birds flew, in and out
    the windows, with delirious wings,
    and the roof beams tremored under
    the hammer blows
but the floor held.
          One by one he
    picked up the books
              and read,
the gongs and old bronze bell sounds
    rolled in the air
    against the door—
and the door held
    in the tremor of room—
    supporting each other.
And we held the poet at the podium
    and we held together
and he spoke and the words flew in
  and out the tremor of air
    and we caught them
      and we held.

POEM FOR YOUNG PEOPLE I KNOW

(According to the Bible, Jacob, fearing death from his brother, fled. But an angel wrestled him all night and Jacob did not let go until the angel blessed him. Then Jacob was able to cross over the river to meet his brother and make peace with him, and both lived.)

"I am the angel of death,
the password is mine. Let me in!"
The angel of death said
to the poet who stood in the door. "No!"
said the poet, "for here
I am the keeper of words
all words."
And she gathered into her hand—
sweeping syllables and vowels and
consonants mixed
in the palm, and said, "every word I need
for the poems of young people I know
writing their way through all dread,
who need these words to live."
"One is mine!" Said the angel of death. "Give
it to me!
Word that is key I use to take from life
whatever child I choose!"
"Then I wrestle you for it!" The poet
cried, "that all of the children live!"

But death laughed into the silence
"Psalms, phrases, rewrite them all—
whatever most amazes
still answers to death's call.
And my wings wring sinew from socket
my strengths wrench tears from eyes!
I take endings of meanings—the moving
finger wrote on the wall—
what I know is all."

Then those wings whipped up and down in air
  like the strokes of a pen
wing spread wider than condor's
the six great wings, in ever wild revolutions,
she wrestled all night long,
and every letter held.
Wingspan stronger than eagle
          that tears asunder flesh.
Wings tossing billows of feathers like thick foam
  spraying.
    Wings in voluptuous darkness,
voice like a tongue of fire as if falling, falling,
  through sea, and the giant tentacles
          binding, but
  it was only a dream of the sea.
  No dream the stretching tendons,
  the far-outreaching pinions.
Wings which astounded the winds,
          sending vibrations
  shuddering against the galaxies.
But she felt the curve of the earth solid
under her feet. With deepening dips in the soil
where her heels dug in—as she held,
holding all the syllables tightly.
    She had gathered nouns, pronouns,
          adjectives.
"I am keeper of the door,
  holder of all the consumate words
  that give us ecstasy.
Words that tell who we are and of
the act of wonder.
  I see these words a-tangle
  in the sensitive neural system,
all of the nerve ends tremble
to the stimuli of sound,
    and the human fetus respond
    in the heartbeats-rhythmic-move,
the whole evolving mind becoming articulate,

and infinite perceptions
receptive to words.
I delight in language of joy of life!
Never one of my words can you
use against me or mine.
Must I wrestle you through the darkness,
must I hold you at bay all night?
I hold you until you bless me!"
Holding all the syllables tightly
so her people could make their poems,
she called under the rush of wings—
Words they needed for their life.

(In one California city where high school age young people in trouble are given the choice of jail or school, they choose a school whose name in translation means "to life". Records show, nevertheless, that by mid-term at least one student dies, often by his/her own hand. This poem is written about and dedicated to Carol Henry-Dennis, who has worked hard to change that statistic.)

CHANGE OF WORLDS

(Chief Seattle's speech to Isaac Stevens, Governor of Washington Territory, 1854: ". . . there is no death, only a change of worlds . . . ")

It is our turn, tangled in tendrils together,
hair and grass alike, to be layers on this earth.

Around, above us, concentric circles of
insects,   revolving patterns of wind,
are in the world's slow circle, turning.

Who will first rise to go—know if to go is to rise
or   be lowered to roots, felt under surface of skin.
We have not seen the other side of the grass.

"Where has she gone?" they will ask.
      "She was here
in this circle with us   on the earth
with the grass stem's juice on her tongue."

She is in the circling of the bee   and in
the circular current of wind—the same
and not the same   as the wind of last September.

I THINK OF THE SEA IN ITS OTHER WORLD

What has sea created in its other world
where whales hear with their bones,
and books, dropped into water, rot?

Created things, and gave them up to air,
and neither hair, nor fur for the cold,
but lashless eyes, returned from light,
    to hold stark images.

Not things with fingers.
Forms whose teeth are sharper.
Oysters that are mute fat tongues
    in dark.
Textures layered between bone and scale.
Shapes that understand their impulses, and
thought apart from sound.

And I could love it, love it and live there,
wordless,
holding my breath   forever.

Then the slow worm pulls its length from earth,
from below earth.
That happens, and I think again
of all the other worlds I do not know.

Mary Rudge has won critical acclaim in the *San Francisco Examiner* and other newspapers as one of the Bay Area's most charismatic poets. As an organizer of Oakland's first festival of literary arts and many other community arts events, she is known as an arts activist, as a "cultural catalyst" and has been cited by the mayors of Oakland and Alameda for cultural achievement.

She also has had wide experience as a multimedia poet having performed and exhibited at Bay Area museums, galleries and colleges, and on TV and radio.

She has appeared abroad at events in Spain, Morocco, Holland, France, and also in Mexico. With The Poetic Dance Theater Company of Artists Embassy International, she has performed on three continents and in several states in the U.S.

In 1985 she was awarded the Honorary Doctorate of Literature from the World Academy of Arts and Culture, Taipei, along with poets Thor Vilhjalmsson of Iceland and Osten Sjostrand of Sweden; in 1984 she was awarded the title of Princess of Poetry from Academia Italia Della Arte, Rome; and in 1981 her work was chosen for award by the World Congress of Poets.

She has co-edited an international women's peace anthology and the biannual *Poets and Peace International.* Congressman Fortney Stark read her poetry into the Congressional Record in 1982 as a salute to the ongoing effort to promote world peace through the arts.